BEGINNER'S INTRODUCTION TO PRIVACY

Special Thanks

A huge thank you to the NBTV team for their work on this book: Tanya, Will Sandoval, Reuben Yap, Ogre, Lee Rennie, Kieran Mesquita, Chris Karabats, Sam Ettaro – Their research and efforts with this book, towards helping people empower themselves in the digital age are so valued and appreciated.

Thank you to Marta Belcher and the Filecoin Foundation for their expertise and assistance in looking over this book as we put it together. Also thankful for their own efforts towards helping create a more private world.

Thank you to all the builders who are trying to create a more private and decentralized future.

Thank you to all of the readers, for caring about privacy and reclaiming freedom in your digital life. You will help us change the narrative of society

Table of Contents

Introduction To Privacy In The Digital Age

This book is an introduction to privacy in the digital age. To understand why this is an important topic, one must only look around them at current events.

After Russia invaded Ukraine, Tor and Signal users spiked because suddenly citizens realized that protecting their privacy in a hostile situation was critical.

In Iran there have been mass protests against authoritarianism. In response, the parliament voted in an overwhelming majority to execute the 15,000 protestors they had arrested. These executions have already begun[1]. Protestors are increasingly aware of how important it is to protect their privacy when voicing dissent against the government.

Around the world, people are regularly thrown into the limelight overnight when something they say unexpectedly goes viral. They hadn't realized their home address is all over the internet, and now the safety of their family is at risk.

---

[1] https://www.amnesty.org/en/latest/news/2022/12/iran-horrifying-execution-of-young-protester-exposes-authorities-cruelty-and-risk-of-further-bloodshed/

These are big examples that can show us the consequences of a tightly connected world where privacy is an afterthought.

We shouldn't wait until the situation is dire to learn how to use privacy tools. These are things that we should all be familiar with now: Not only is a time of crisis a terrible time to be learning new tools, but it also might be too late by then.

But privacy isn't just about safeguarding against some unlikely yet catastrophic event in the future. It's about protecting ourselves from very real and constant threats in our present. These threats can be hard to see, because the internet is a very abstract idea to many people. Hopefully this book will shed some light on why privacy is more important than we realize.

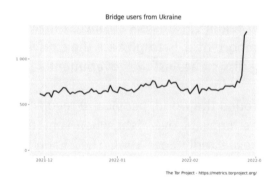

Bridge users from Ukraine

The Tor Project - https://metrics.torproject.org/

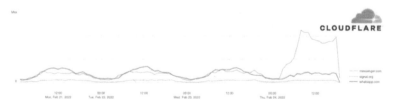

CLOUDFLARE

Privacy Is An Iterative Process

Privacy is not absolute. And it's not an end-game. It's an ever-evolving process. Most people don't want to hear that. They like quick-fix solutions. They want to take a pill, or buy a product, and their problem will be solved. That's just not how privacy works.

Let's say you "fix" one area of data leakage in your life. If someone really wants to target you and get your data, they'll iterate and find new ways to get it. So privacy becomes like a game of whack-a-mole, and that's why people find privacy so difficult. They're looking for an airtight, complete solution.

The question is, DOES someone actually want to target you? For most of us, the answer is no. This means that we can get a long way just by making simple changes in our lives, and these will have a huge impact on our privacy. The more "at risk" you are, the more careful you have to be and the more layers you need to add. Determining your risk profile is something that only you can do. You'll have to look at what you want to protect yourself from, and how much convenience you're willing to sacrifice for that protection.

It's important to ask the question: what kind of surveillance am I worried about? Am I being targeted specifically? Do I just want to avoid general corporate surveillance? Am I looking to carve out the most freedom in my life? This is called *analyzing your threat model*, and this will come up repeatedly throughout this book as we provide different options for people that vary in security and convenience according to what your threat model is.

So where do you lie on this spectrum of privacy vs convenience?

Privacy As A Spectrum

On one end of the spectrum are the people who have a house filled with smart devices like smart thermometers, security systems, an Alexa, they use SMS and Gmail for everything, and have a phone with countless apps that they carry around with them everywhere they go. Sound familiar?

On the other end of the spectrum are the people who tell you that the only way to protect your privacy is to throw out all your digital devices and live in a forest, inside a faraday cage, disconnected to the outside world. Not using the internet is certainly one way to reclaim your digital privacy. But where's the fun in that?

There is a middle ground for the average person. None of us want to throw out our computer and phone. The internet is awesome and we should be able to participate in this wonderfully interconnected world without feeling like we're sacrificing all of our privacy by doing so. Even in this middle ground, there are varying degrees of privacy to aim for, which again depends on your threat model and willingness to sacrifice convenience for privacy.

Are you being targeted by someone? You're going to need extreme privacy measures. We give some pointers on where to find those tips in a moment. It's worth noting that extreme privacy is very difficult, and requires you to sacrifice big conveniences in your life. Most people who aim for this either really know what they're doing, or they get burnt out pretty quickly.

If you're just starting out on your privacy journey, you should be aware that privacy fatigue is a very real thing. I advise you to make one small change at a time, and not be overwhelmed with all the ground there is to cover. This book focuses on the simplest changes you can make that have the biggest impact on your life. Even if you only make a few of these changes, you're still decreasing your digital footprint and should be proud of your effort, because it all makes a difference.

The Cracks In The System

Snowden once said:

> *"It is, in a dark way, psychologically reassuring to say, 'Oh, everything is*

monitored and there's nothing I can do. I shouldn't bother.' The problem is that it's not true."[2]

We think of surveillance as a single, monolithic system that we can't evade. It's actually the result of countless different systems. Not only are there cracks between these systems, but these cracks can be learnt by privacy-conscious people. In this book we aim to teach you about some of the highest impact things you can do to begin your privacy journey.

It's important to understand that each layer of privacy you add isn't bulletproof, but we'll show you how to layer solutions, to give yourself the best possible chance to maintain your privacy in the digital age.

Understanding The Tech We're Using

Most of us don't understand the tech we're using at all.

Why would we? We're not all software developers, or network engineers.

---

[2] https://twitter.com/Snowden/status/1546790812704440322

The joy of using modern tech is that we don't have to understand it to use it. I don't have to know how my computer works to be able to turn the power button on and check my email.

We as a society have taken down barriers to entry and made life-changing technology accessible to everyone.

But there is a danger in using things that we don't understand. We're making tradeoffs that we don't even know exist.

This isn't a computer science book. We're not going to dive into the nitty gritty complexities of how computers work. But we are going to give you enough information that you can make more informed decisions in your life.

This book is not to persuade you to stop using certain products and services, it's to make you aware of how these products and services might be harming you, so that you can make your own decision about what's best for your life. This way we can be more empowered human beings.

Further Resources

I have done a lot of reading and researching over the years that has formulated my views on privacy. Here are some of the things that have inspired me on my journey, which you should dive into if you want to learn more about how to protect your privacy online:

Books

Extreme Privacy - Michael Bazzell

This book is a monster read. It's technically dense, very thorough, and constantly updated with all the latest research and tools. If you decide to dive deeper into the privacy rabbit hole, this is a must-read. It's geared towards people who are willing to go the extra mile to protect themselves online. Even if you're not ready to implement some of the suggestions made, it's really informative about how your data is being collected and what you can do to stop it, and absolutely worth the read.

Permanent Record - Edward Snowden

A great overview of how the internet landscape has changed over the last 20 years. We've moved from transient beings that are allowed to change and evolve, to having permanent records chronicling our every action and thought. Snowden provides a beautifully eloquent argument for why we should all start protecting our privacy, and explains why he upended his life to fight for this cause.

No Place to Hide: Edward Snowden, the NSA, and the U.S. Surveillance State - Glenn Greenwald

A journalist's perspective on the importance of free speech, and how privacy plays a crucial role in this. He dives into the Snowden revelations, where he was part of the Pulitzer prize-winning teams that first presented them to the world. The story from his perspective is fascinating, and he paints a chilling picture of where we could end up if we lost privacy in our everyday lives.

Podcasts

Darknet Diaries[3]

Educational and terrifying podcast filled with true stories from the dark side of the internet. If you want to understand the threats that are out there for ordinary people, listen to this podcast. They're fascinating stories where each episode reads like a thriller, and you'll learn a whole lot.

The Privacy, Security, and OSINT Show[4]

Hosted by Michael Bazzell, this is a great supplement to his book "Extreme Privacy". Technology is constantly changing, so be sure to listen to this podcast for regular updates on all his extreme privacy measures.

---

[3] https://darknetdiaries.com/

[4] https://inteltechniques.com/podcast.html

Websites

Freedom of the Press Foundation[5]

They provide great resources geared towards helping people like journalists protect their privacy. It's great information that applies to all of us.

The Electronic Frontier Foundation (EFF)[6]

They have great guides and tools online, as well as explainers to help you protect your privacy online.

Your Personal Privacy Journey

Finally, there are all kinds of reasons why you might be reading this book. Everyone has a different privacy journey, everyone is at different stages, everyone has different circumstances in their life that led them here.

This book is for everyone.

Perhaps you want to better protect your young daughter from a hostile world where she doesn't yet understand the consequences of her digital actions.

---

[5] https://freedom.press/

[6] https://www.eff.org/

Perhaps you don't like corporations sharing your data with thousands of other companies and making huge money from your personal and sensitive information.

Perhaps you're concerned about the mass surveillance of governments, because even if you trust your government today, you might not tomorrow. Regimes come and go, but that data is forever.

Perhaps you're traveling to a country where you're concerned that they might not be friendly to someone in your situation.

Perhaps you want the ability to communicate with your loved ones privately.

Perhaps you want to become a more empowered individual, who makes more informed choices, and you want your technology to work for you instead of the other way around.

Whatever led you to begin your privacy journey: Welcome.

Privacy is normal, and an ideal worth fighting for.

Surveillance isn't inevitable. Let's stop normalizing it, and let's take our lives back.

Important Note

While all the information in this book was accurate at the time of publication, technology changes fast. We plan to release new editions of this book that will not just include relevant updates, but will include additional chapters so that you can continue to expand your privacy journey.

You can also keep an eye on our channel[7] for the latest information.

This is a beginner's guide to privacy, and great for anyone who is not sure where to start. Once you feel that you've got a good grounding in the topics we've covered and want to advance to more complicated and sophisticated privacy techniques, we highly recommend trying out some of the other resources we suggested above.

---

[7] https://www.nbtv.media/

CHAPTER ONE:
WHY AND HOW?

Why Is Privacy Important?

Let's start with why privacy is important. Not everyone is convinced that it is. There are many excuses I hear online:

"I'm not particularly interesting, so who cares what I'm doing online?"

1. Oh, but you are interesting. Your data is analyzed by data scientists in ways you can't even imagine, and is monetized by more people than you imagine. What you think isn't important, is actually fueling a hundred-billion-dollar, data-brokerage industry, and you're a part of it.

2. Unfortunately, surveillance doesn't care whether you're interesting or not. Your data is hoovered up indiscriminately, by companies, by governments, by hackers. The issue though is that it's all stored forever. So if there's a chance you might one day become interesting, you might want to start thinking more about digital privacy. Otherwise you're allowing the contents of your life to be picked over at any time in the future, by any future adversary.

"I have nothing to hide, I'm not doing anything illegal."

1. Snowden said it best when he said that laws change, societal norms change, regimes come and go, but that data is forever.

You may feel safe now, but in 10 years someone else might be in power who doesn't make you feel so safe, because situations change. They will have this permanent record about all your online activities, and they will be able to use that information for any purpose of their choosing.

If you think there's a chance that you might disagree with something a future government does, you may want to rethink how you protect your digital life.

2.   We sometimes presume all laws are good, but throughout history we've overturned countless bad laws. Civil disobedience is an important way for society to reevaluate norms and adjust regulations accordingly.

How could people have realized that marijuana could help people with debilitating seizures, and the nausea caused by chemotherapy[8], without first trying marijuana?

Whatever your own personal views, there are almost surely laws that have existed in the past that you don't agree with. Those laws could not have been changed without good people willing to fight to get them changed.

---

[8] https://www.mayoclinic.org/drugs-supplements-marijuana/art-20364974

In a perfectly obedient society we can't test out theories and push back against bad laws. It's a sterile environment that doesn't allow dissent.

The point is that we must continue to fight for a better society, according to our values, regardless of whether someone has given us permission to do so. And it's possible that in an increasingly surveilled society, dissent becomes increasingly difficult.

How Data Collection Works

Protecting our privacy starts with understanding how data collection works.

Our data is overwhelmingly able to be collected because we voluntarily hand it over.

We choose services that have access to all of our emails, and we give them permission to scan and analyze our inbox.

We opt for products that explicitly tell us they're going to share our data with third parties, and we click "agree" anyway.

We give companies permission to use our data to feed their algorithms.

This is great news, because it means that if we make better choices, we can make a huge difference in our online privacy. We can swap out products and services for more privacy-preserving options.

Now perhaps you're in the camp that doesn't care about companies using our data, and are more concerned about potentially dangerous regimes creating profiles on all of us with this data. Governments largely collect our information the same way, through these private companies to whom we voluntarily give our data.

Let's explain:

Governments don't need to build new infrastructure to collect data if, for example, Google has already built that infrastructure, and we voluntarily give Google data.

But doesn't the government need a warrant to access this data about us, in most of the world?

Not necessarily, and the details of this depend on where you are in the world.

Third-Party Doctrine

In the USA, for example, there's something called the "Third-Party doctrine".[9] It's a rule that says people who voluntarily give information to third parties have "no reasonable expectation of privacy". This is a disaster for the digital age, because everything we do online relies on third-

---

[9] https://en.wikipedia.org/wiki/Third-party_doctrine

parties. We use third-party servers, third-party browsers. To even access the internet means you're relying on some company's underground cables.

It's a pretty outrageous rule, because that's just not how expectations of privacy work. You wouldn't expect anyone that's babysitting for you to be collecting information about what you have in your house. Nor would you expect someone to be recording your private conversation with a friend over coffee, or for them to try to sell you products related to that conversation.

But that's how governments and companies alike justify digital surveillance and data collection. They say that this data you hand to third parties no longer has the constitutional protections that it would have if you kept it in your own home. So your personal finances that your bank sees, your home address and phone number you give to a website, the entire contents of your email, messaging, and SMS history: All of these are fair game. Companies can use this information about us. They can hand it over to governments if they want, and those governments don't even need subpoenas to get it, if the company is happy to hand it over of their own volition. Most companies are: they don't want to get on the bad side of regulators, so they hand over information freely. There are also no meaningful privacy regulations to protect this data in the USA, but even in countries where there are privacy regulations, they're impossible to enforce uniformly. Laws that are enforced arbitrarily are problematic.

Sometimes governments even have direct access to these companies' servers to query data when needed, through programs like the PRISM program. We know very little about the PRISM program, and most companies that are involved in it have denied granting this access to the government. Once the government gets this data, it's stored in permanent databases attached to our identity.

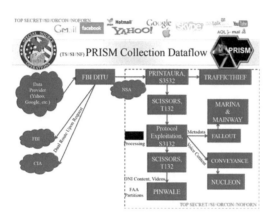

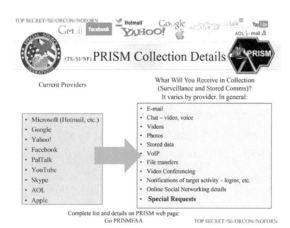

The point is that it matters what information we hand over to companies, because it ends up in all kinds of hands all over the world. Companies can sell it to thousands of other companies, it's compiled by data brokers and passed into more hands, sometimes companies just don't secure our data properly and it falls into the hands of hackers and adversarial nation states. Safeguarding our information in the first place is tremendously important.

This is how the bulk of our data is actually collected, because we voluntarily hand it over.

The thing is, most of us don't realize this is a choice we're making. Some people don't realize there are more privacy-preserving products and services we can choose instead. They don't realize they can use masking tools to hide activity for their ISP. Or tools to hide their financial choices from their bank. Or messaging apps that don't reveal the contents of the message to anyone, except the sender and recipient.

So now we're going to dive into some of these tools, explain which ones are the best for privacy, so that you can make more informed decisions in your digital life. Choosing to swap out products and services that intentionally limit the amount of data they can collect about users is a great first step to minimizing intrusion into your privacy.

Here are five areas we'll cover:

- Web Browsers
- Search engines
- VPNs
- Email
- Secure messaging

CHAPTER TWO:
WEB BROWSERS

Web browsers are the gateway to the internet, so they have the potential to collect huge amounts of data about us. With almost all major browsers claiming privacy features, it is important to know which of them truly protects us.

How is privacy leaked in browsers? Many ways.

Website Cookies

Let's start with cookies and how they help websites track us.

Cookies are small bits of text that are downloaded to your browser that act like storehouses of information, and contain things like website preferences, language settings, or login information. You can think of them as a way to "mark" a visitor of a website in order to recognize them and their settings later on.

PowerShell   Copy
```
Set-Cookie: session-id=1234567
```

PowerShell   Copy
```
Set-Cookie: session-id=1234567; max-age=86400; domain=example.com; path=/;
```

Cookies themselves can be very helpful, doing things like remembering your login or preferences across different sessions. But some cookies help companies track you across multiple websites.

For example, Facebook uses cookies and trackers embedded in other websites such as the "Like" and "Share" buttons that appear on shopping, news and other sites. Even if you don't use these buttons, Facebook can use them to determine which sites you visit and tie them to your Facebook account.

Website Fingerprinting

Another more subtle way your privacy can be breached is through browser fingerprinting: Websites can detect your unique environment such as your operating system, browser, your screen resolution, timezone, and many other data points. These data points combined together form a unique identifiable fingerprint even if cookies are blocked.

Browsers Breaching Your Trust

Not only can websites track you, but browsers themselves can also send back information about you to the browser's parent company. They can record all your traffic, reveal details about your device, or even send your keystrokes when you type into the search bar. In other words, your browsers become spies for the likes of Google or Microsoft and send all this information back to them to monetize. Three of the biggest offenders are Google Chrome, Microsoft Edge, and Yandex.

Chrome

Google Chrome has a staggering 65% market share[10, 11] of the browser market. It is made by a company whose primary business is making money from collecting our data, so it is predictably poor on the privacy front.

Chrome is also not open source – there are parts of the code that are not public, so this makes it hard to know all the ways it is capturing your data. Here are some things to keep in mind about Google in general, when browsing the web:

We are persistently prompted to link our Google accounts to Chrome the moment we log in to any Google service. This is not just for your ease of use -- all activity on your browser becomes linked to your Google account once you click that button.

Google's default settings are set to allow tracking until you delve deep into the settings to disable them. It's a maze of tracking that is almost impossible to untangle. As The Independent reported in 2020, "Google's privacy settings are so

---

10 https://backlinko.com/chrome-users

11 https://www.statista.com/statistics/268254/market-share-of-internet-browsers-worldwide-since-2009/

confusing even its own engineers couldn't turn them off, lawsuit shows".[12]

Even using its autocomplete feature in Chrome's search bar sends data to Google. When you start typing something into the search bar, it doesn't even matter if you don't click enter and never actually search for it, that unsent data is still sent back to Google.

Google has been talking for years about eventually blocking third-party cookies. These allow third parties to track you across different websites, and every other major browser has stopped allowing them years ago, but Google keeps kicking the can down the road. Their latest announcement at the time of publication said you could expect these changes mid 2023. We'll see if that happens. [13]

Even if this change eventually occurs, Chrome never said that they wouldn't stop tracking you, just that they're going to use the data differently. They will still keep track of a user's browser habits across the web and will use this data to place you into various "cohorts" that will allow advertisers to target you.

[12] https://www.independent.co.uk/tech/google-privacy-settings-engineers-location-tracking-phone-a9691046.html

[13] https://www.theverge.com/2021/6/24/22547339/google-chrome-cookiepocalypse-delayed-2023

Microsoft Edge and Yandex

Microsoft Edge does block trackers from sites you haven't visited by default and has several preset profiles from basic to strict to easily adjust your desired level of protection. But it was classified as a particularly egregious privacy-offender in a 2020 study[14] from Trinity College in Dublin.

> *Excerpt: "From a privacy perspective Microsoft Edge and Yandex are much more worrisome than the other browsers studied. Both send identifiers that are linked to the device hardware and so persist across fresh browser installs and can also be used to link different apps running on the same device. Edge sends the hardware UUID of the device to Microsoft, a strong and enduring identifier that cannot be easily changed or deleted. Similarly, Yandex transmits a hash of the hardware serial number and MAC address to back end servers. As far as we can tell this behavior cannot be disabled by users. In addition to the search autocomplete functionality (which can be disabled by users) that shares details of web pages visited, both transmit web page information to servers that appear unrelated to search autocomplete."*

---

[14] https://www.scss.tcd.ie/Doug.Leith/pubs/browser_privacy.pdf

Safari

Safari fares better. Safari blocks third-party cookies by default and has built-in Intelligent Tracking Prevention (ITP) that is designed to identify advertisers and other parties that attempt to track your online activities, and remove the cross-site tracking data left behind.[15]

However Google researchers have found that ITP may actually leak user's web browsing habits. While Apple has published fixes for these, Google's researchers maintain that the fixes do not solve ITP's underlying privacy issues.

Safari is produced by Apple, which does a lot of good stuff for privacy. If you use Safari on iOS and have a paid iCloud account, you can take advantage of their private-relay tool (we will dive into that in our section about VPNs vs Tor). In general for the average person, this is going to be a giant step up from using something like Chrome.

However if you want even better privacy, there are other options you can look at.

Brave, Firefox and Tor Browser are leading the charge with privacy.

---

[15] https://research.google/pubs/pub48871/

Brave

Straight out of the box, Brave is a great browser for privacy. It requires less tweaking and customizing of settings than other browsers to get you to a strong level of privacy. So if you're after something that is really good for privacy and is plug-and-play this is a great option.

It blocks ads and search autocomplete by default, so you don't have the issue of keystrokes being sent back to a search provider such as Google before clicking enter on your search.

They also block more unwanted advertising and tracking links than any other browser right out of the box. If you're using Brave, it doesn't matter if you click on a link with a bunch of stuff after the question mark.

Eg:

https://twitter.com/naomibrockwell/status/152 2345817549545474?s=20&t=IE5PjCLO1byiMbNTbVw IWw

The string of characters after the question mark in most URLs is often tracking you. Brave will automatically strip out that part of the URL before navigating you there.

You know how when you go to certain websites, and before getting there, in the bottom left of your browser you'll see a bunch of different URLs quickly appear?

This is called bounce tracking, and it's a way for a whole bunch of different companies, data brokers, and advertisers to track which websites you're going to. Brave combats this by learning over time which particular link type is always bouncing you through these tracking websites first, and instead just takes you straight to the final destination rather than through these tracking pages first. This is called Debouncing and Brave has the only version of this that ships in the browser.

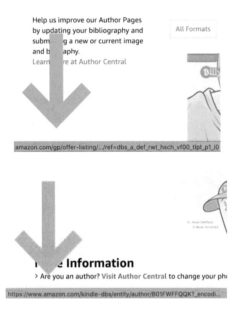

They also do something called Unlinkable bouncing, where these tracking websites are visited in a throwaway storage area where no identifiers are present. The tracking domains never build up a profile of you because Brave throws away storage for it every time you leave it. So next time you come back, the tracking site won't be able to know that it was the same person who visited. Brave has the most aggressive version of Unlinkable bouncing that ships in the browser.

They also build anti-tracking tools that target specific companies, like Google and Facebook. Many browsers just build universal protections around

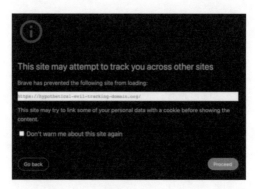

general concepts, and every policy is applied to everyone on the web. But if Brave knows Facebook is doing a very specific kind of tracking, they build tools that specifically target Facebook's measures, and are not afraid of putting them in a box that they wouldn't put on a normal website.

Firefox

Firefox is also great for privacy, because they have a wide variety of extensions that can further protect you. For example, Facebook container is a Firefox extension that creates a boundary between Facebook and the rest of the web to make it harder for Facebook to track you online. Firefox also has an official extension called Multi-Account Containers that extends the container feature to other sites, to help you keep parts of your online life separate. For example, you can use them to silo your shopping, banking, or work, without having to clear your history, log in and out, or use multiple browsers. Making Firefox super robust for privacy does require tweaking settings and tinkering, but many people like having that kind of control over their browsing space.

Firefox is also one of the few browsers that doesn't use the Blink browser engine, which is made by Google. Browser engines help your computer turn website code into what you see on screen. Google's Blink engine has more than a 70% market share. Having a single dominant browser engine actually makes developers' lives a lot easier. But if Blink becomes too dominant, developers might stop testing their websites on other engines and not bother with cross compatibility. This gives Google immense influence in dictating web standards, and could make it even worse for privacy down the road. Firefox uses the browser engine Gecko.

Tor Browser

If privacy is of the utmost importance, Tor browser is the best choice. Tor browser is a stripped down and hardened version of Firefox that routes all its connection through the Tor network, encrypting your traffic and hiding your real IP address.

Tor stands for The Onion Router. It's a network comprising thousands of servers run by volunteers that protects your privacy by hiding your IP address and activities on the internet.

A very broad level on how it works: When your internet traffic leaves your computer, it's wrapped in multiple layers of encryption. Instead of going straight to your destination, it bounces around many different servers on the TOR network first, and at each server, a layer of encryption is removed. It's like peeling an onion, hence the name, "Onion routing".

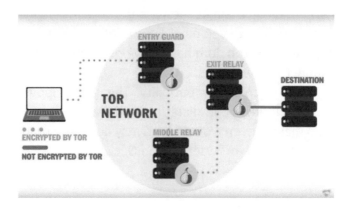

This means that no server that received your traffic is aware of the full route of the traffic. The gateway (the first server you reach, that allows you to enter the Tor network) knows you're the one sending a request, but they don't know what the request is because they're not allowed to read it. The relay servers don't know anything about the traffic that they're bouncing around because it's all encrypted. The final Tor server, called an exit, knows exactly what's being asked for, but they don't know who's asking for it.

To use this network is easy, just download the Tor browser. This is NOT a tool for everyday usage though. It is slow, and not suitable for high bandwidth activities such as video streaming. It's also a tool that can be used to access the deep web, but you should be very careful about this because it can be an unsafe place for your computer.

It's also useful to know that while Tor hides what you're doing on the internet from your ISP, it doesn't hide the fact that you're using Tor. Tor traffic has a distinct signature that can be identified and certain countries have used this to block Tor usage. Even where Tor is allowed, the usage of Tor can make you stand out to ISPs or government agencies. There are ways to try and hide this traffic signature, but that's the subject for a more in-depth guide to Tor usage.

While Tor isn't perfect, it's an essential tool for anyone in a higher risk position, such as a journalist, whistleblower, activist, or even just someone who wants to go the extra mile to protect their privacy.

Others

There are many other privacy-focused browsers that people might recommend and they might be worth taking a look at if it's recommended by someone you trust. We've focused on the browsers that have the most dominant market share.

Personally, I like things to work well right out of the box and require the least customization from me in order to make it more private. You can make your choices according to your personal preferences.

If you're using Chrome, making the switch over to another browser like Brave or Firefox will go a long way to protecting your privacy.

CHAPTER THREE:
SEARCH ENGINES

A lot of people get confused between browsers and search engines. If a browser is the car you're driving to get to websites, the search engine is the map you're following that shows you where everything is.

The most popular search engines out there today are Bing, Baidu, Yahoo, and of course by far the most used search engine, Google.

They are like directories that list all the websites that exist. You just type in keywords, and they will show you a list of websites that match your criteria.

Although today we take them for granted, having a directory of addresses completely revolutionized how we access the web. You used to have to know the exact URL of something in order to find the page, and with the advent of search engines this was no longer the case. There's a great moment in the show "Halt and Catch Fire" where Lee Pace's character starts collecting URLs by hand[16]. Every time someone tells him a new URL, he'll put it on a post-it note and add it to his collection. The earliest indexes were all manually-created lists like this, where people had collected their favorite websites from across the internet and put them all into a curated directory. In fact, the first website I ever made was a list of Australian Bands' websites, curated in a single page so that people could access them easily via a hyperlink.

---

[16] "Halt and Catch Fire" Season 4, dist. AMC Networks

These days, all these URLs are indexed not by hand, because that would be completely impossible, but by bots that crawl the web like spiders.

A web crawler is a program that automatically searches the internet by following links from one web page to another, with the goal of indexing the entire web.

These web crawlers are super important for search engines. A good search engine has usually had an army of these bots scouring the internet for a long time, and has built a comprehensive index of every nook and cranny of the internet it can find.

When choosing a search engine, it is important to consider:

- How good is their index?
- What are the chances that they have indexed the site that I'm looking for?
- Will I be able to easily find what I'm looking for?

But another incredibly important consideration is

- How private is the search engine?

Search engines have the potential to be massive data collection tools. Your search queries provide a deep, granular insight into who you are as a person, including your interests, medical concerns, political views, and sexual preferences. Search engines like

Google collect every keystroke you enter into the search bar, even if you never actually go through with a search and press enter. The characters you type and then delete are all being sent to Google's servers anyway, and that's how they're able to autofill suggested searches for you. Search engines also have the ability to collect other information about you, like your IP address, location, information about the web browser you're using, unique identifiers to your machines, and browser cookies.

The purpose of this data collection is two-fold.

1) the more a search engine knows about you, the more personalized the search results can be, and the greater chance that they're able to know what you're looking for, and show it to you.

2) the more a search engine knows about you, the more money they make.

Google, for example, is often thought of as a search engine company, but they're actually an advertising company. The more they know about you, the more money they can charge to put advertisers in front of you. So there's a big tradeoff that can occur between convenience and privacy when these search engines collect information about you.

The flip side of filtering results to show you the most relevant information is that they can filter results to influence or manipulate you, and also censor information This is another consideration to be aware of when choosing a search engine.

Psychologist Robert Epstein coined the term "The search engine manipulation effect", and conducted studies calculating that "Google has the power to flip upwards of 25 percent of the national elections in the world with no one knowing this is occurring."[17] [18]

There have even been studies that show how autofill in search engines can be used to strategically manipulate people. [19] [20] [21]

If you type in:

"NBTV is..."

and your search engines autofills

"... complicated, boring, dangerous ..."

---

[17] https://aeon.co/essays/how-the-internet-flips-elections-and-alters-our-thoughts

[18] https://spreadprivacy.com/google-filter-bubble-study/

[19] https://lincolnpolicy.org/2020/in-algorithms-we-trust-the-story-of-google-search/

[20] https://www.wsj.com/articles/SB10001424052970203347104578099122530080836

[21] https://www.wsj.com/articles/how-google-interferes-with-its-search-algorithms-and-changes-your-results-11573823753?mod=hp_lead_pos10

you're going to get a very different immediate first impression than if it autofills:

"... empowering, educational, fun ..."

And by filtering the results you're shown, search engines can control narratives and the flow of information. Take the iconic photo called "Tank Man". You've probably all seen it. Tank Man shows an unknown person blocking a line of tanks in Beijing, the day after the Tiananmen square massacre in 1989. The image is banned in China, but is well known in the rest of the world.

On June 4 2021 (the 32nd anniversary of the Tiananmen Square Massacre), if you had performed an image search for "Tank Man" using the search engines Bing, Ecosia, Yahoo Search, DuckDuckGo, and many others, you would have returned no results.[22]

"There are no results for tank man. Check your spelling or try different keywords."

How is that possible, when the image is so famous? All of these search engines rely on Microsoft's "Bing" index for their search results, and for some reason *(*probably entirely unrelated to the Tiananmen Square massacre anniversary that day, of course)*, Microsoft decided not to allow the western world to see that image.

Bing responded that this was "due to an accidental human error and we are actively working to resolve this", and the image soon reappeared. But this does demonstrate the incredible power that search engines wield to either promote certain information or hide information. So it's important to choose your search engine wisely, based of these three considerations we've mentioned:

- Quality of Indexing Tools
- Privacy
- Filtering policy

---

[22] https://www.theregister.com/2021/06/04/search_engine_tiananmen/

Let's dive into some specific search engine options.

Google

Almost 90% of internet searches in the United States use Google.

Google has become such an important part of our lives that we turned their name into a verb: *"Don't know the answer? Google it."*

Obviously people wouldn't use Google unless there were good things about it, but it's important to know what the tradeoffs are so that you can make a more informed decision.

The Good

Their web crawlers are really good, so they're finding sites on the internet that other crawlers might not have indexed yet. If you're looking for something in particular, it's possible Google will give you the best chance of finding it.

The Grey

Google knows you intimately, and they severely filter the results they show you.

This means that they can make a really good guess about what you're looking for, and show you the most relevant results. They're able to predict what you're actually looking for in your searches, and they prioritize those results on top while hiding less relevant results.

This also means that what you're shown is carefully controlled. [23]

In fact what you're looking for may actually be hidden from search results.

"They're showing me millions of search results, isn't what I'm looking for just in later results pages?"

Not necessarily. Google actually hides results.

You know how when you perform a search on Google, it will say: "About 405,000,000 results (0.77 seconds)"

Google doesn't actually show you over 400 million results – they will choose a subset of those results to show you. That's an important consideration to keep in mind when choosing a search engine: is that search engine showing you what's actually out there, or what they want you to see?

The Bad

Google is awful when it comes to privacy. They're collecting everything -- your unsent keystrokes, your queries, your location data.

---

[23] https://spreadprivacy.com/google-filter-bubble-study/

Everything they know about us gets fed into their advertising machine.

One of the biggest steps you can take for your privacy is to stop using Google search engine – because remember, this data isn't just staying with Google. It's shared with thousands of companies, governments, data brokers, and more.

Alternatives

When choosing an alternative, there are 2 categories of search engines you can choose from:

- Pure search engines
- Meta search engines

Pure Search Engines

Pure search engines have their own web crawlers, and they build up their own index of results.

Google is widely regarded to have one of the best web crawlers, or spiders, for generating search results. Google's crawler, called Googlebot, is designed to quickly and efficiently crawl the web and index web pages, allowing users to search for the information they need. However, Google is a privacy nightmare, and heavily filters results. There are alternative pure search engines that provide unfiltered, uncensored search results, allowing users to access a wide range of information from the web. There are also some options that also respect the privacy of their users. The trade off is that most web crawlers haven't indexed as many sites as the behemoth Google has. This means that you can notice a deterioration in the relevance of results.

Meta Search Engines

Meta search engines do not generate their own search results, but rather rely on the results from other search engines and databases. They gather results from these sources into their own list of results. These are useful because you can get the benefit of, say, Google's search results, but have them delivered to you in a more private way.

It is not necessarily the case that all meta search engines are better for privacy than pure search engines, but there are some options that strip tracking links from results, provide archived pages for you to view instead of letting websites know that you're looking at their page, and refrain from collecting IP addresses or building a profile on you.

The downside is that these results from the meta search engine will still be subject to whatever censorship and filtering Google has in place (or whichever engine they're pulling their results from).

Other

There are also hybrid search engines that both trawl the web for their own results and also mix in results from other sources.

So to summarize, the search engine you choose will depend on what you prioritize. Here are three pillars we are considering when recommending search engines:

Three Pillars
- Quality of Indexing Tools
- Privacy
- Filtering policy

Ideally you can find a search engine that has the best of all these worlds,
Here are some of the privacy-preserving options that you can explore

Brave Search

Brave Search is what I use in my setup. It is a search engine developed by Brave Software, the company behind the Brave web browser. Brave Search is designed to prioritize privacy and security, and it does not track or collect user data or search history.

They say on their website:

> *"First, and most important, Brave Search adheres to core principles of privacy. We don't track you, your searches, or your clicks. Ever. This is far different from the vast majority of search providers, who siphon up every piece of data about your search behavior, and tie it directly to you."*

Brave isn't quite a metasearch engine or a pure search engine, according to the common understanding of those terms. They are closest to a pure search engine, but they do things a bit differently. Brave has their own index and Brave Search returns almost only results from Brave's search index, with (if necessary) a shrinkingly small amount of results from other, non-Brave sources.

However, they don't use crawlers to add sites to their index. Instead, Brave users can volunteer to contribute to the index based on the sites they visit. This system is opt-in, and is called the "Web Discovery Project."[24] Because your browsing history is sensitive, there are a lot of protections in place and precautions taken before they decide to add a page to their index. This is mainly done through a system called "STAR." [25]

It stands for "Secret Threshold Aggregation Reporting", or the longer name, "Secret Sharing for Private Threshold Aggregation Reporting" and you can read their official documentation (whitepaper) on their website.[26]

It's a general technique that allows a server (like Brave's) to only see a value (like a URL) if it's been shared by multiple users. This ensures that Brave never learns about websites unless they've been visited by a lot of people (so they're not uniquely identifying). They also never see the IP addresses (or other identifying information) about information contributed from Web Discovery Users through STAR. This system won the "distinguished research" award at the ACM Conference on Computer and Communications Security[27] (probably the top research conferences in the field) and they've open

---

[24] Web Discovery Project

[25] https://brave.com/research/star-secret-sharing-for-private-threshold-aggregation-reporting/

[26] https://brave.com/research/files/star-ccs-2022.pdf

[27] https://www.sigsac.org/ccs/CCS2022/

sourced[28] the system and are proposing it for standardization in the IETF.[29].

They operate their own, independent search index that lists billions of web pages, which means they're not beholden to the censorship, biases, or economic interests of the larger search indexes out there that most people rely on. Although they have their own index, they can also anonymously check their search results against third-party results, and mix them on the results page. For full transparency they provide a "Results independence" metric which shows the percentage of search results that come from Brave versus these third parties.

When delivering their results, Brave allows you to choose for yourself how you'd like your results to be filtered through their beta "goggles" feature. This allows you to create a set of rules for how your results should be ordered when delivering to you. This means that instead of a single ranking of results, Brave offers almost limitless ranking options. You could choose your own political leanings, prioritize content from "tech blogs", remove Pinterest pages or copycat content. You are far more in control of the algorithms dictating what you see.

Their website says:

> "While Brave Search doesn't have editorial biases, all search engines

---

[28] https://github.com/brave/sta-rs

[29] https://datatracker.ietf.org/doc/draft-dss-star/

have some level of intrinsic bias.
Goggles allows users to counter this
intrinsic bias in the ranking
algorithm."

You will see different search results depending on your own filter settings.

Overall, Brave Search is a good option for users who are concerned about their privacy and security when using search engines. It offers a unique and private search experience, along with some additional features and benefits.

DuckDuckGo

Another popular search engine alternative is DuckDuckGo. They are a mix of pure search engine and meta search engine: They have their own crawler (the DuckDuckBot), and also compiles results from other sources, mainly Bing. DuckDuckGo has historically had two major pillars for their platform: respecting privacy, and removing the "filter bubble". They have written extensively in the past[30] about the dangers of allowing Google to influence what you click.

---

[30] https://spreadprivacy.com/google-filter-bubble-study/

However in 2022 they announced that they too would start filtering results according to what they think users should see. [31]

This met backlash from the community.

It is worth noting that all algorithms have their own bias, and people can manipulate these algorithms to boost their rankings. So just because no one has manually intervened in search results, it doesn't mean that search engine is more factually accurate. The problem many saw with DuckDuckGo's behavior though was that their main marketing push for many years was "unbiased results" that provided an alternative to Google's filter bubble. We feel they no longer fit this criteria,

[31] https://twitter.com/adam3us/status/1502023044478418947

and for that reason we no longer promote DuckDuckGo.

MetaGer

MetaGer is an open-sourced, privacy-focused search engine service, provided by the German non-profit organization SUMA-EV. It uses the hybrid model of combining the search results from its own web crawler with those of other search engines. MetaGer has 24 small-scale web crawlers under their control, and they relay search queries to as many as 50 search engines to supplement results. These results are filtered, compiled, and sorted before being presented to the user.

It allows users to search the web while protecting their privacy, by not storing any personal information about its users, such as their IP addresses or search history. Additionally, it uses encryption to protect the privacy of users' search queries, and it allows users to opt out of certain types of tracking, such as the use of cookies.

MetaGer has an integrated proxy server that allows you to view websites anonymously: the receiving website and other third parties only see MetaGer's proxy rather than your IP address.

It's also available as a hidden TOR service for maximum privacy, and it doesn't use any tracking cookies.

It also provides users with a variety of options for customizing their search queries, making it a versatile and effective tool for finding information online.

Searx

Searx is a privacy-focused metasearch engine that allows users to search the web without being tracked. Searx does not collect or store any personal information about its users, which helps to protect their privacy.

It's a metasearch engine that sources its results from other search engines such as Google, Yahoo and Bing, Searx makes sure it does this anonymously and does not share users' IP addresses or search history with the_search engines from which it gathers results. Tracking cookies are also blocked.

All search results give you a direct link to the respective site, rather than a tracked redirect link and, when available, these direct links are accompanied by "cached" or "proxied" links: The "cached" links point to saved versions of a page on archive.org, while the "proxied" links allow viewing the current live page via a Searx-based web proxy.

This allows you to see the results pages without having to visit the sites themselves with your unique identifiers.

It is an open-source project, which means that anyone can contribute to its development and help to improve it. This makes Searx a more community-driven and transparent search engine than many others.

As an open-source project, Searx can be downloaded and installed on a personal server, which allows users to run their own instance of the search engine. If you want to really ensure that the search engine isn't logging your data, self-hosting can be a great option. This also gives the user more control over their search experience. To self-host Searx, you will need to have a server with a Linux-based operating system and the necessary dependencies installed. You can then download the Searx code from GitHub and follow the instructions in the Searx documentation to set up your own instance of the search engine. Note that self-hosting Searx requires some technical knowledge and may not be suitable for all users.

Searx also provides users with a variety of options for customizing their search queries, making it a versatile and effective tool for finding information online.

Yacy

Yacy is a decentralized, peer-to-peer search engine that allows users to crawl the web and build their own search index. It is designed to provide an alternative to traditional search engines, which are often centralized and controlled by a small number of companies.

There is no central server, but instead thousands of servers in multiple countries providing results. This means that YaCy results can't be censored, and they can't be subpoenaed to provide your search history, because there is no central authority that can provide this.

In terms of its effectiveness as a search engine, it has received mixed reviews. Some users report that it can be slow and lacking in the breadth of content that is available through more mainstream search engines. Ultimately, whether or not Yacy is a good search engine will depend on your individual needs and preferences.

Startpage

Startpage is essentially a more private way to use Google search. Based in the Netherlands, it is designed to provide users with a more private and secure way to search the web, as it does not collect or share personal information about its users. It uses the same search results as Google, but without the tracking and personalization that Google is known for, and they don't store any search data.

They have an anonymous view browsing feature, like Searx, which allows users to search the web by proxy and not reveal unique identifiers. They are also constantly innovating with apps users will be familiar with from Google, but which are crafted to protect their privacy. Some examples include a Private Language Translator, Private Stocks Search, Private Currency Converter, Private Shopping, and a Region Filter to let users customize their search results.

There has been some controversy over Startpage's funding and whether it conflicts with their promise of privacy. In 2019, they received a considerable investment from Privacy One Group, a subsidiary of System 1, which is an advertising company.

Although it seems strange that a data collection company would give a large sum of money to Startpage, the Startpage CEO clarified: [32]

> *"System1 is interested in Startpage's ad revenue, not its data. … The reason a company like System1 openly owns other search engines and consumer tech products like Info.com and Mapquest is that they want to capture that ad revenue that is slowly shifting to private search engines. There has been a steady increase in people using private search engines and therefore a steady increase in their revenue. It is a growing market that they feel will continue to thrive and grow. … In no*

---

[32] https://www.computing.co.uk/news/4017337/privacy-focused-search-engine-startpage-details-system1-investment

way does System1 want to change the privacy practices or process by Startpage, in fact, they legally cannot as all of those decisions are held by the co-founders of Startpage. "

These reasons seem to make sense to me, so it's a product that I use in my privacy toolbox.

Qwant

Qwant is a hybrid search engine that is based in France. It is designed to provide users with a more private and secure way to search the web, as it does not collect or share personal information about its users. Qwant also has a strict policy against tracking and profiling, and it does not allow any third-party advertising on its platform. In terms of privacy, Qwant is generally considered to be a good option. It provides a high level of protection for its users' personal information and is committed to respecting their privacy.

It has three unique home pages to begin a search.

Search queries are also encrypted and your IP is also disassociated from your searches.

Like other privacy focused search engines, Qwant doesn't use your search history to help you deliver results as it doesn't retain user data, which is good, but also means your previous searches aren't saved or remembered which is the sacrifice made for the additional privacy.

It is to be noted that Qwant does share some anonymized data with Microsoft to deliver contextual advertising based on your region and what you type into search.

I don't use Qwant, for the same reason that I don't use DuckDuckGo: They advertise a more neutral point of view instead of trapping users in a filter bubble, but have recently begun filtering results according to politics.

While I understand why companies might choose to filter their results in certain ways, I disagree with those same companies advertising that they are "neutral" while doing so.[33] The lack of honest, self-awareness is a red flag to me.

Mojeek

Mojeek is a search engine that is based in the United Kingdom. Their search results come from their own index of_web pages, which has been created by_crawling the web. Mojeek has already indexed over 4 billion pages and retains its commitment to be independent from big tech. It also interestingly has an 'emotional' search function where it categorizes content using deep learning to five different emotions: 'love', 'laughter', 'surprise',

---

[33] https://twitter.com/qwantcom/status/1498755728877801472

'sadness' and 'anger' allowing users to for example filter out sad news items.

It is designed to provide users with a more private and secure way to search the web, as it does not collect or share personal information about its users. Mojeek also has a strict policy against tracking and profiling, and it does not allow any third-party advertising on its platform. It provides a high level of protection for its users' personal information and is committed to respecting their privacy.

Mojeek doesn't implement user tracking and IP addresses are stripped and replaced with only a country code. The only time it does record your IP address is if the search query relates to illegal and unethical practices relating to minors.

Like other pure search engines on this list, Mojeek's strength is also its weakness. Without relying on other search engines, it can claim to be more independent from the big companies such as Google or Microsoft but it also means that search results may not be as ideal but our own experiences demonstrated reasonably accurate results with quite a different emphasis than Google or Microsoft.

Presearch

Presearch is a decentralized, open source search engine that is built on blockchain technology. It is designed to provide users with a more private and secure way to search the web, as well as to give users more control over their online data. Presearch uses its own proprietary search algorithms and index to provide search results, rather than relying on other search engines' results. This means that Presearch is not a meta search engine, which is a type of search engine that retrieves and displays results from multiple other search engines. Instead, Presearch is a pure search engine that generates its own search results.

In terms of its effectiveness as a search engine, Presearch has received mixed reviews. Some users have found it to be a useful and efficient tool, while others have reported that it can be slow and lacking in the breadth of content that is available through more mainstream search engines.

Summary

Many of these search engines do a lot of the same things and the reason why you might select one over another could literally be as simple as liking one small feature more than the other. So try them out and see what you like. It's really easy to stop using Google for search queries, and it goes a long way to protecting your privacy.

My Setup

First, I switched out the default search engine used in my URL bar. Many browsers are set to Google as the default, and privacy-conscious people don't want to use them. In your browser, under preferences, you can select a different search engine for the URL bar. There are usually a limited number of alternatives you can select.

I use Brave Browser, and in that browser they set Brave Search as the default search engine for the URL bar. I keep that setting (we'll give details on Brave Search below). I've found that 99 times out of 100 Brave Search will provide me the information I'm looking for. You can also find their search engine at the address search.brave.com. In Brave you also have the option to set the default search engine to other privacy-focused search engines.

I then set my homepage to a different search engine. I like Startpage.com, but you can choose which option you enjoy the most.

Now when I search, I can either open a new tab and search via Startpage's homepage, or type my query into the URL bar and use Brave's search engine. Sometimes if I don't get the results I'm after on Brave, using Startpage is a great way to supplement my search, or vice versa.
I've had a really great experience with both.

CHAPTER FOUR:
VPNs

VPN stands for Virtual Private Network, and it's a private network within a public network like the internet, to connect remote sites or users together.

It sounds complicated, but basically you can think of it like a private tunnel inside of the internet. When your traffic leaves your computer, instead of going straight to the site you want to visit, it goes through this tunnel first, and emerges to the internet through the VPN's servers instead of through your own personal device.

This has many different use cases.

First of all, someone might set up one of these virtual private networks for their employees who work remotely, so that they can access the work's local network securely. This provides a secure way for them to tunnel into the office's private network.

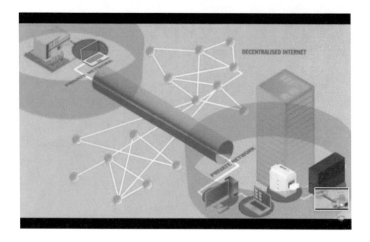

Next, VPNs use encryption to secure the connection between your device and the VPN server, ensuring that any data sent through that private tunnel is kept private and protected from third parties. This is useful for anyone who wants an extra layer of protection on their internet usage. One use case would be if you're using public wifi in a café on an unsecured network. Someone malicious might be on that public wifi network, intercepting your traffic. If that traffic has been encrypted by the VPN software before it leaves your computer, even if someone is able to intercept it before it gets to the VPN server, they won't be able to read it.

Another use case would be to hide your activities from your Internet Service Provider, or ISP. ISPs are notorious for selling data about customer internet activity, but a VPN is helpful for improving your privacy in three ways:

1) Protecting Data in Transport

VPNs wrap your traffic in encryption, so that even if it's intercepted, it can't be read.

This isn't as important as it used to be, because these days most websites on the internet use HTTPS (Hypertext Transfer Protocol Secure). HTTP is the primary protocol used for transferring data on the web. It sounds complicated but basically means that when you look at the URL of the site you're visiting, it starts with "http://". This traffic is not encrypted in transport, which means that if someone intercepts your traffic, they can read it. Then HTTPS came along, that is a secure version of this protocol, and DOES encrypt your traffic. This is where the start of the URL begins with "https://". HTTPS uses encryption to secure the connection between your web browser and the website you are accessing. This is especially important for websites that handle sensitive information, such as online banking or shopping sites, because it keeps things like your credit card details private.

As the internet has matured, most websites have now adopted the HTTPS standard to make sure that people visiting their websites can do so securely.

Even though most traffic is HTTPS these days, some isn't, and a VPN can still provide protection in those cases.

2) SNI Hiding (Complicated explanation)

Even for HTTPS traffic, in many cases your browser still shares the domain you're communicating with in the clear (even if the rest of the traffic is encrypted). This is because of SNI (Server Name Indication), which is usually sent in the clear, so that, if a single server is handling traffic for multiple domains, the server knows which TLS key to use for the HTTPS session. There is a fix for this, ECH (Encrypted

Client Hello), but it's not widely supported yet, so a VPN is important here.

2) SNI Hiding (Simple explanation)

Your ISP can often still see the domain you're visiting, because your browser usually indicates which hostname it's attempting to connect to at the start of your session, and this can be visible even when the traffic is encrypted with HTTPS. So a VPN is important to hide the hostname.

3) Obscuring IP Address

Even when you're using HTTPS, and even in cases where there isn't an SNI problem, the ISP can see the IP addresses you're communicating with. This will often reveal which sites you're visiting, because many websites will have a static IP address. A VPN can prevent this, because the ISP will only see the IP address of the VPN server you're passing your traffic through.

One thing to keep in mind when using a VPN is that you're essentially just transferring trust from your ISP to the VPN company. There are a few reasons why this is probably warranted. As mentioned, ISPs are your worst enemy when it comes to privacy because of their track records with data selling.[34, 35]

Next, an ISP usually requires all kinds of identity verification to set up your internet connection. In contrast, it's possible to sign up for a VPN anonymously, paying with cash or crypto. Keep in mind that if law enforcement wanted to connect you to this VPN usage, with most VPNs there are ways to subpoena the company and get your IP address.

So when using a VPN, it's important to remember that this isn't a tool for anonymity, it's a tool for privacy. It allows you to choose better methods of using the internet that will give you the greatest chance of improving your privacy and mitigating data leakage.

34 https://restoreprivacy.com/internet-service-providers-isp-privacy-data-collection/

35 https://cdn-resprivacy.pressidium.com/wp-content/uploads/2021/10/FTC-ISP-Report.pdf

If you choose a good one, they can be tremendously helpful for privacy, and I highly recommend using them for all your internet activity, on your phone and on your computer.

Not All VPNs Are Good

What I'm about to say might turn you off VPNs completely, but please stick with me. Because, as I mentioned, a VPN is an essential tool in your privacy toolbox. But you HAVE to make sure you choose a good one.

It turns out that an overwhelming number of VPNs are actively harvesting and selling your data, capturing passwords, credentials, and movements from your web activities, and doing all sorts of awful things.

There is a dark underbelly to the VPN world that most people don't want to talk about.

Malicious activity

Many VPNs are just a shell hiding a data collection scheme.

Be especially wary of free VPNs. A good question to ask yourself is "how do they make their money?" If it's not obvious, they're probably making money from your data.

A cursory glance at various app stores will show a plethora of "free VPN apps".

It's very likely that the reason these apps exist for free is because they're data-collection tools that are making money from collecting your information. It's a service that's paying for itself: a dual-purpose app.

Take 1clickVPN browser extension for Chrome for example. It apparently has 3 million users, and is doing a bunch of malicious activity.

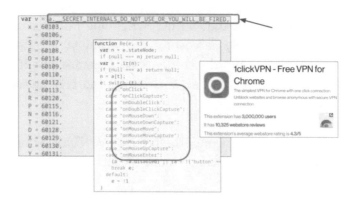

Looking at the code you can see that there are instructions telling the VPN to capture things the user is doing, like monitoring keyboard activity and mouse movements. There are many VPNs that will collect these things, like what you're typing, how fast you're typing etc.

Almost always, the user has no idea this is going on.

Things like mouse movements are useful to malicious companies because it helps them create more effective botnets for one. These bots are trying to mimic human behavior, so there are VPNs that literally steal this human behavior so that it can copy them.

With most VPNs you won't even get to see what's in the code. When we are able to decompile code and inspect it, the code might not even tell us if something malicious is happening – the malicious activity might be happening elsewhere, like in the server process, or in some obscure library that the code is referencing. This is how many of these malicious apps get past certain security checks for apps stores – because the code that the app store is looking at isn't doing any malicious activity... but the servers are. So the dangerous app just sits in the app store enticing potential users, and we have no way of knowing if the reviews are even real or fake. App stores are filled with empty shells of apps that are never updated, but just left there hoping to attract users and collect their data.

```
(window.webpackJsonp = window.webpackJsonp || []).push([
  [2], {
    "+215": function(t) {
      t.exports = JSON.parse('{"name":"chainstart","comment":"Start of the Ethereum main chain"
```

Some of the code we analyzed also made reference to the "Ethereum main chain". Why would a VPN need to be doing anything blockchain related? One potential reason is that they're using your computing power to mine cryptocurrency.

But that doesn't mean that all paid VPNs are safe. Whether it's a free or a paid VPN, there are additional ways to make money from the people using it. And these companies are making money hand-over-fist. There's a lot of money in the VPN industry.

Copycats

Then there are a bunch of VPNs that are just ripping off other free VPNs or free proxies. As soon as there's one VPN service, it's a publicly accessible VPN that anybody can use. So a malicious actor can come along and just use the same network. Or sometimes they're actually the same provider, and they just have different front ends for their product, and each different version is just sitting there collecting data for any user it attracts. There's no real way to know unless one deeply investigates, and that might take months if not years, because it's incredibly difficult.

Security Concerns

Data collection isn't the only thing you need to be careful of. Sometimes the security of these VPNs is really poor. Many services that call themselves a VPN are actually just a proxy server.

Similar to VPNs, proxy servers establish connections on your behalf and also protect your IP address from the end party.

However, proxy servers are not always encrypted, which allows your internet traffic to be intercepted and analyzed. So a lot of these VPNs aren't providing any security for your traffic, they're just hopping your traffic through a different access point.

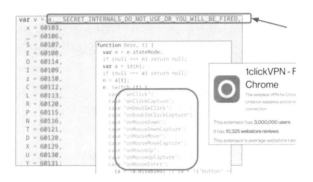

There are also VPNs that hard code secret internals into their source code, which is a huge security concern.

```
}, {
key: "sync",
value: function() {
    var e = this;
    fetch("https://".concat(a, "/api/v1/checks/auth")).then(function(e) {
        return e.ok ? e.json() : Promise.reject()
    }).then(function(t) {
        e.storage.signed = !!t.ok || e.storage.signed, e.saveStorage()
    }).catch(function() {}), fetch("https://".concat(a, "/api/v1/servers/")).then(function(e) {
        return e.json()
    }).then(function(t) {
        e[](t[], t]) !== e[](n[], e.storage.servers)) && (e.storage.servers = t, e.saveStorage(), e.setProxy())
    }).catch(function() {})
}
}, {
```

```
{
    "countryCode": "LT",
    "countryName": "Lithuania",
    "cityName": "Siauliai",
    "nodes": [
        {
            "host": "lt.iclickvpn.net",
            "ip": "93.115.28.101",
            "port": 443,
            "schema": "HTTPS"
        }
    ],
    "credentials": {
        "username": "VTpt",
        "password": "n4gb
    }
}
```

Some even hard code in the username and password to the VPN server itself. That means that anyone who looks at the code can actually see the login credentials for accessing that server. There are lots of ways someone could cause a LOT of havoc with access to this server.

App Permissions

Be careful which permissions an app requires in order to run.

Some of these might include device ID, call information, phone status and identity.

Location permissions are frequently requested, but a VPN doesn't need location in order to work efficiently. It also doesn't need wifi connection information, storage. A VPN doesn't need bluetooth information in order to run, so when an app asks for it, it seems very data brokeresque.

We don't know why apps need these permissions, but one possible reason if we read between the lines is that they want to make extra money somewhere.

VPNs actually need extremely minimal requirements in order to run efficiently. If your VPN is requesting unnecessary data, it should be a big red flag.

Granted there can be other reasons why these apps need those permissions, for example some apps allow you to auto-connect to their VPN when on an untrusted network, for which they request location and WiFi permissions.

Or there are apps that will nudge users to turn off their bluetooth when not using it, to prevent bluetooth tracking, for which they need bluetooth permissions.

There's no way to confirm that these companies are doing what they say they're doing, but that doesn't mean they're automatically nefarious either. These are just good questions to ask when downloading apps, to make sure you understand why they're asking for certain permissions. If you want to be safe, choose a VPN that requires minimal permissions in order to work.

No Logs

You will see a lot of companies claim that they have a "no-logs" policy. Unfortunately there is a lot of fraud in this area in the VPN industry. In 2020, Comparitech found 7 Hong Kong-based VPNs that had "no logs" policies, and were actually collecting logs including account credentials and potentially user-identifying information.[36]

The problem with "no logs" claims is that you can't prove a negative. As CNET said,

> *"Verifying that a VPN isn't logging user activity is impossible from the outside. That's why some VPNs hire external auditors -- or even journalists -- to check inside their networks and see if they can find anything amiss. It's a nice idea, but even once you're rummaging through internal servers, not stumbling across a trove of logs doesn't mean they aren't there. "*[37]

VPNs require a lot of trust to use. Some companies have a better reputation than others, so we'll at least give you a couple of options.

---

[36] https://www.comparitech.com/blog/vpn-privacy/ufo-vpn-data-exposure/

[37] https://www.cnet.com/tech/services-and-software/why-you-should-be-skeptical-about-a-vpns-no-logs-claims/

Other Ways VPNs Misrepresent Their Product

Research from Consumer Reports indicates 75 percent of the most popular VPNs

> *"... inaccurately represented their products and technology, or made hyperbolic or overly broad claims about the kinds of protection they provide their users."* [38]

Tag lines like this are incredibly common with VPNs:

> *"Unrivaled internet anonymity!"*
> *"Keep all prying eyes at bay!"*
> *"Stay untraceable and anonymous online!"*
> *and*
> *"Safe from hackers and snoopers!"*
> *"Turn yourself digitally invisible!"*
> *"Military-grade encryption!"*

Let's take a look at that last one: military-grade encryption.

Consumer reports says:

> *"Many security professionals say that this term should be a red flag for consumers, because it doesn't*

---

[38] https://www.consumerreports.org/vpn-services/vpn-testing-poor-privacy-security-hyperbolic-claims-a1103787639/

really mean anything. There is no one standard form of encryption used by the military."

A VPN is not a panacea, and it's not bullet proof. Be careful of companies that misrepresent what their products can actually achieve.

Also keep in mind that a lot of a VPN's transparency is self-reported and hard to verify. If you catch a VPN provider lying about one thing, it's probably a good idea not to trust any of their claims.

Choosing a Good VPN Location

Both the location of the VPN server and the parent company can be important. For example Switzerland is a great place for VPNs. Within the current Swiss legal framework, the government there is unable to compel VPN providers to start logging IP addresses. However, if the company is in the US, but the server is in Switzerland, the VPN company can still be compelled to turn over information.

There are some countries such as India that require VPNs to report all the activity of their users, and hand over logs to law enforcement.[39]

---

[39] https://www.cnet.com/news/privacy/india-orders-vpn-companies-to-collect-and-hand-over-user-data/

Even if the country has "no-log" policies by default, many governments (such as the US, Panama, and the British Virgin Islands) can actually put pressure or even force VPNs to log as the result of a direct order. In the US this can be done through things like a National Security Letter.

While good VPN jurisdictions vs bad VPN jurisdictions are worth considering, they should also be taken with a grain of salt.

There are many complex alliances for sharing data between countries, like mutual legal assistance treaties.

EU countries have sharing agreements for data, the 5 eyes (an alliance comprising the UK, US, New Zealand, Canada, and Australia) do also. But even if a country is not a member of the 5 eyes, or the European Union, there is a lot of cooperation between law enforcement of different countries for handing over data, so many people question how helpful the location of a VPN is at the end of the day.

Your own location can also be very important when choosing whether to use a VPN.

1. North Korea — Illegal
2. Iraq — Illegal
3. Belarus — Illegal
4. Oman — Partial; illegal for individuals
5. China — Partial; unauthorized VPNs are illegal

6. Russia — Partial; illegal when used to access blocked content
7. Turkey — Legal but heavily restricted
8. UAE — Legal but restricted
9. Iran — Legal with some restrictions

Using a VPN in a country where it's illegal can actually make you stand out more. Be careful.

Which VPN Should I Use?

Unfortunately, there is no definitive source where you can check if your VPN is safe and private.

We're all doing the best we can with our research, and there are no guarantees. However, one VPN company that has a great reputation almost universally in the computer security community is Mullvad.

It is an open-source VPN based in Sweden that uses the WireGuard and OpenVPN protocols. Mullvad accepts Bitcoin, Bitcoin Cash, and Monero for payment in addition to conventional payment methods, and they also accept cash, which is a great way to have even more privacy in your usage. Mullvad is known for its strong emphasis on privacy and security, and it does not collect or log any information about its users' online activities.

Remember companies change their products, and new research is being conducted all the time that changes the standards of what is considered "secure". So keeping up to date using resources like freedom of the press, EFF, or privacy tools is a good idea.

Privacy expert Michael Bazzell also recommends ProtonVPN, especially from a stability standpoint with whole network VPNs. Computer security researcher Jonathan Tomek gives a great overview of VPNs in his Defcon presentation from 2022. Thank you to him for lending us some of his research for this piece

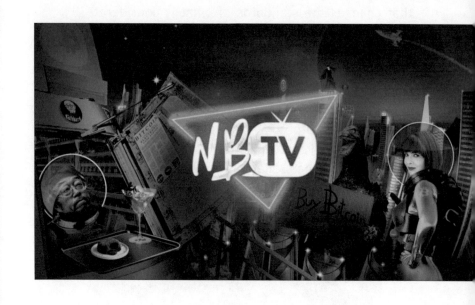

CHAPTER FIVE:
EMAIL

Email is an essential backbone of internet communications with over 4 billion users worldwide.

But it's not private.

Snowden says:

> *"Email is a fundamentally insecure protocol that … can and should be abandoned for the purposes of any meaningful communication."* [40]

Edward Snowden ✓
@Snowden

⋯

I would not (and do not) use email, except as throwaways for registration. Email is a fundamentally insecure protocol that, in 2019, can and should be abandoned for the purposes of any meaningful communication. Email is unsafe. I'd use @Signalapp or @Wire as a safer alternative.

11:52 AM · Sep 21, 2019

This is because email wasn't designed with privacy or security in mind. In its original form, email was transferred completely in the open, everything was readable by anyone who watched network traffic and there were little to no checks to prevent impersonation. But as email's importance grew, instead of overhauling the way it works to provide

---

[40] https://twitter.com/Snowden/status/1175437588129308672

security and privacy, various protocols were layered over to try and address these issues.

Most of us are not going to stop using email. But there are things we can do to increase our email's privacy. Ideally you can find an email provider that meets the following criteria.

- Retain minimal metadata
- Zero-access encryption
- End-to-end encryption

First, they should collect and retain minimum metadata and personal information about you. You don't want an email provider that is keeping a database of all this information.

Next there's Zero-Access Encryption: this means that your email and attachments are encrypted while stored so that even your e-mail provider can't read them. Zero-access encryption prevents the messages in your mailbox from being shared with third parties or leaked in the event of a data breach. But encryption and decryption still happens by the email provider and there is a split second in which the message is accessible to the email provider before it is encrypted.

Finally, end-to-end encryption which takes things a step further than zero-access encryption.

Instead of just storing emails in an encrypted way, encryption and decryption of e-mails happens entirely on a user's device so that whatever information the email provider receives is already encrypted. This means that the content of your email is only readable by the sender and recipient. No one else, not even the email provider itself, can get access.

Let's dive into specific services and whether a privacy-conscious person should be using them.

The Bad: Gmail, Yahoo, and Outlook

Gmail has 1.8 billion users, making up almost half of the entire email market share.[41]

Other popular and free email options are Yahoo and Outlook.

The entire content of your emails are visible to the likes of Google, and Yahoo and they use this data to build profiles of you and feed their algorithms

Google claims that it no longer reads emails for the purposes of *advertising*[42] BUT they still actively use your email to learn more about you, train their

---

https://saasscout.com/statistics/gmail-statistics/

[42] https://variety.com/2017/digital/news/google-gmail-ads-emails-1202477321/

own artificial intelligence, and they even let third-party developers have access.[43]

Microsoft now offers end-to-end encryption for outlook, when you send an email between outlook users, but they can read everything sent to and received from providers outside of outlook.

You can make a HUGE difference to your online privacy by switching away from these email providers.

Two popular and more private alternatives are ProtonMail and Tutanota. I use both and I like both for different reasons.

The Good: ProtonMail

ProtonMail was one of the pioneers of zero-access and end-to-end encrypted email. They also have lots of useful features such as dedicated mobile apps, encrypted address books and calendars. They have free options and they have paid options, and the user experience is very similar to Gmail.

Let's understand how they're handling encryption, so you know just what kinds of privacy you're getting by using this service.

---

[43] https://www.thesun.co.uk/tech/7312296/google-read-gmail-emails-snoop/

End-To-End Encryption

To lock down an email's content with end-to-end encryption (e2ee) and make it only accessible by the sender and recipient, these 2 parties need to agree on a digital lock and key.

If you send an email from your ProtonMail account to someone else's ProtonMail account, this is easy, and ProtonMail automatically end-to-end encrypts these emails.

When the sender and recipient are using different email providers, it becomes more difficult.

There are 2 ways that ProtonMail allows you to end-to-end encrypt your email if you send an email from your ProtonMail account to someone's email with a different provider:

The first is using something called a PGP key. This is more technically complicated, and requires the contact on the other side to know how to use PGP and have a PGP plugin installed in their mail client already.

The second way to secure your emails, which is super easy, is with password protection. You simply add a password to the email when you're composing it.

The recipient will need this password in order to read the message, so ideally you would share this password with them using a different secure communication channel.

The recipient will receive an email telling them they have been sent a secure encrypted message. They'll be prompted to enter the password, and this will take them to a secure ProtonMail mailbox where they can read your message and respond using E2EE. They don't need to have a ProtonMail account to do this.

These password-protected emails also have a self-destruct timer you can set, so the email is only visible for a certain period of time, and after which it will be automatically deleted.

This tool protects the emails you send from the prying eyes of your recipient's email provider, even if they're using something like Gmail.

Zero-Access Encryption

ProtonMail also makes sure that they put incoming emails from other providers outside of their own reach, using zero-access encryption. The biggest benefit to this is that if ProtonMail's servers ever get hacked or compromised, no one will be able to get access to the contents of your emails, and ProtonMail can't hand over access to your emails to anyone because they don't have access themselves.

Keep in mind if an email is sent to you from Gmail, Gmail still retains a copy of that email that they can access, but ProtonMail won't have an accessible copy.

One thing to keep in mind is that the subject lines in ProtonMail are not end-to-end encrypted, and this is because ProtonMail adheres to the OpenPGP standard. PGP, short for Pretty Good Privacy, is an encryption system that has become the de facto standard for encrypting emails. In PGP, the subject line is part of the header packet which is not end-to-end encrypted. By adhering to OpenPGP, Proton Mail isn't just a standalone service, it becomes compatible with a larger encrypted ecosystem though work is being done to update the OpenPGP standard to support encrypted subjects.

ProtonMail is a very popular, privacy-focused email provider, popularity is important: If more of your contacts use ProtonMail, more of your emails are being end-to-end encrypted by default. There is a network effect in getting those around you to use the same email provider as you.

The Good: Tutanota

Tutanota is another popular email provider that prioritizes privacy. Like Protonmail, there are free and paid versions and it has a comparable feature set: support for encrypted calendars and contacts. It does fare slightly better in its privacy policy: while it does collect metadata which it destroys after seven days, it doesn't log IP addresses by default. Though strangely, if you use Tor or a VPN it may log that IP address. The official reason it gives is that it considers such information already anonymized and therefore no longer 'personally identifiable information.

Tutanota also automatically end-to-end encrypts all emails sent from a Tutanota account, to a Tutanota account. They also store all emails with zero-access encryption, putting these stored emails outside of their own reach.

A benefit that Tutanota has over Protonmail is that the subject of email is also encrypted. This is because they do not support OpenPGP standards.

The drawback of this is that you can't use PGP to end-to-encrypt your emails with people outside of the Tutanota ecosystem. They do, however, allow you to password-protect emails with a pre-agreed upon password, the same way Protonmail does.

Other Options

There are quite a few niche email options if you're looking for privacy, though they tend to be much more barebones and lack the polish of Protonmail or Tutanota. They're also more oriented towards tech savvy people. To name a few: Posteo and Elude.in, Riseup, and Countermail.

What some of these services provide over Protonmail or Tutanota are less metadata retention and some even have support for Tor onion services. They still employ zero-access encryption so that even they don't have access to your emails however, unlike Protonmail or Tutanota, many don't offer integrated and seamless end to end encryption and instead rely on users to deal with PGP or plugins like Mailvelope to do it.

Switching your email provider away from something like Gmail and towards a more privacy option is an essential part of your privacy journey. Email is not a very secure way to communicate, but using a privacy-focused option can help.

It's worth reminding you that so much of the privacy world relies on trusting that these companies are doing what they say they're doing, and running the code they say they're running. There is a lot of trust that you're placing on ProtonMail, Tutanota, and these other providers, when they're the ones handling the encryption and decryption of your emails. If you're in a higher risk category, remember that email is an inherently insecure protocol, and seek out more robust communication methods. For the average person, just making the switch away from companies that overtly admit to analyzing the contents of your emails is an important privacy step.

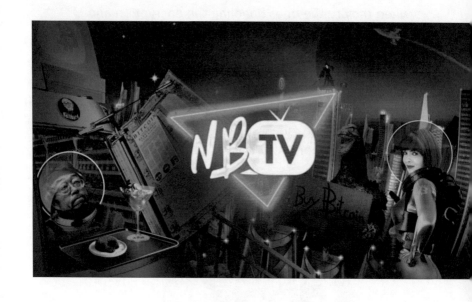

CHAPTER SIX:
PRIVATE MESSAGING

Finally let's talk about our everyday communication using messaging services. There are many popular messaging tools out there, and some of the most popular are the least private.

SMS

SMS (the standard text messaging protocol we are all used to) is a really primitive technology, and not at all secure.

Your messages are not end-to-end encrypted, and they're visible to your cell provider. Cell providers are notorious for selling information about you. They've even been caught selling customers' location data [44]

Sending an sms is like posting a letter to someone in an unsealed envelope, and hoping that no one looks inside. You should avoid SMS because it's not private.

Twitter DMs

Twitter private messages are completely visible to Twitter employees. As was revealed in the recent "Twitter Files" from Matt Taibbi and Bari Weiss, Twitter employees can view someone's private

---

[44] https://techcrunch.com/2019/01/09/us-cell-carriers-still-selling-your-location-data/

tweets as easily as clicking on their "DMs" tab in the dashboard.[45] Don't use Twitter DMs for anything at all in private.

Facebook Messenger

Facebook messenger is not end-to-end encrypted by default. Your direct messages are all visible to Facebook. They have added the option for "secret conversations", which is an end-to-end encrypted option, but even when using that option, a lot of metadata is collected. Facebook uses information from its messenger to build profiles of you and feed their algorithms. Facebook has a track record of collecting a lot of data about its users, so I wouldn't recommend using even their "secret conversations" for private communications.

---

[45] https://twitter.com/bariweiss/status/1601018810495995904

WeChat and QQ

These apps are very popular in China, and heavily surveilled by the Chinese government. Tencent owns both WeChat and QQ. Most users know not to send anything critical of the government through this chat app because there will be consequences. In fact there are tools that allow the government to screen messages before they're sent, and delete them if not approved [46].

In 2016, CitizenLab revealed that Tencent's QQ Browser sent a lot of information about users to Tencent, unencrypted.[47] This lack of encryption was suspected to have been explicitly requested by the government.[48, 49]

It's worth keeping in mind that messaging apps in China need to kowtow to the Chinese government at all times.

---

[46] https://www.privateinternetaccess.com/blog/china-government-can-censor-pics-memes-send-friends-via-im/

[47] https://www.scmp.com/tech/enterprises/article/1931524/if-you-use-tencents-qq-web-browser-your-personal-data-risk-experts

[48] https://citizenlab.ca/2016/03/researchers-identify-major-security-and-privacy-issues-in-popular-china-browser-application-qq/

[49] https://citizenlab.ca/2016/03/privacy-security-issues-qq-browser/

Whatsapp

Whatsapp is the number one messenger app and was one of the first popular messengers to offer end-to-end encryption by default. They turned on end-to-end encryption for over a billion people, and that's awesome. But they are owned by Facebook, and share a bunch of Metadata with their parent company.

It's also closed source, and there's been no publicly available audit.

There was a leaked FBI document that came out last year showing how much metadata law enforcement can legally obtain from different so-called privacy apps, and Whatsapp fared one of the worst. [50]

Telegram

Telegram is often thought of as a private messaging app. This is not true. All messages on Telegram are sent and stored in the clear by default, and without end-to-end encryption this means that they're accessible on Telegram servers.

It is possible to create a one-to-one, end-to-end encrypted chat with someone called "secret chats",

---

50

https://web.archive.org/web/20220104204510/https://propertyofthepeople.org/document-detail/?doc-id=21114562

but almost no one does this because for some reason most people seem to be under the misconception that Telegram is already end-to-end encrypted.

It's not possible to end-to-end encrypt group chats on Telegram.

They've done an amazing job marketing themselves as a privacy app, for a service that doesn't offer this basic privacy functionality.

Even when e2ee is enabled in a secret conversation, they use a home-baked encryption protocol, MTProto. This move has been criticized by experts, because not going with a tried and true cryptographic standard means there could be security holes that haven't been discovered yet. [51]

Recently Matthew Green and Moxie Marlinspike had an interesting back and forth about why Telegram is held up in the media as this private alternative, Moxie himself hypothesized that when Telegram first came out with its insane e2ee standard that all the security experts were so busy talking about that that nobody mentioned it's all plaintext by default.[52]

---

[51] criticized by experts

[52] https://twitter.com/moxie/status/1475501969326309380

iMessage

Another popular messaging app is iMessage, which uses end-to-end encryption for communication between iMessage users. All media and attachments are also encrypted when between iMessage users, and so is FaceTime when you have voice and video calls. You can tell when you're communicating with another iMessage user when your text bubble is in blue. When it's in green, it's an ordinary, unencrypted message.

Metadata is not encrypted, and Apple is known to collect a lot of metadata about their users. iMessage is also not open source, so you have to trust that Apple is doing what they say they're doing.

Signal

The messaging app that I recommend is Signal. It's designed to minimize the data that it collects from users. It doesn't log metadata, it doesn't store a record of your contacts, social graph, conversation list, location, user avatar, user profile name, group memberships, group titles, or group avatars.

Signal has even introduced sealed sender tech that means that if communications were somehow intercepted, the sender's identity is still protected. Heck, even the way it handles stickers protects your privacy.[53]

Signal's software is free and open source and has undergone audits so people can verify that Signal is doing what it claims to do.

My favorite feature is that users can automatically set messages to disappear.

---

[53] protects your privacy

I highly recommend that everyone do this for their messages, and change their settings so that any chat you instigate deletes messages by default. The reason is that most of the time there's no need to keep a permanent record of everything we've ever said to someone. At the end of the day these things are more liability than they're worth, in the event that someone gets access to your phone, or subpoenas it.

Signal isn't without controversy, many people don't like that you use your phone number as your identifier, but if you're interested in extreme privacy options, you can always get another number that's not tied to your name in any way.

Other Options

Some final messaging apps to consider are Session, Threema, and Wire. These are all also great platforms to try out.

Network effect is an important factor when it comes to messaging people, so if no one else in your social circle is using your app of choice, it's not going to be of much use for you, regardless of how private it is. That's another reason why I like Signal, because it's popular: the user interface is so polished that it's really easy to get people to transition to this more private alternative.

Again I'll mention that tech changes, platforms change their policies, so vigilance is necessary in order to make good decisions about your privacy.

Transferring your messaging away from SMS, Facebook, and other social media DMs towards end to end encrypted options is a HUGE step to protecting your privacy.

SUMMARY

If you are just beginning your privacy journey, starting to dive into some of the areas we've outlined in this book is a great way to start out. There's so much deeper that you can go, but don't feel overwhelmed. Be aware of privacy fatigue, and make changes that are going to be sustainable for you. It's ok if you don't do everything at once.

Slowly, you can start to make more conscious and informed decisions in many areas of your life with regards to the tech you use and your privacy.

Your privacy journey is in your hands, and you're more empowered than you realize. Just starting to choose better products, and swap out some of the most egregious data collectors with more private alternatives will go a long way to improving your digital privacy.

Privacy is really important. Increasingly this privacy is being threatened, whether by totalitarian governments intent on sucking up as much data from across the world as possible. [54]

Freedom of speech and freedom of the press are in precarious states right now, and the internet becomes an increasingly hostile war zone with every passing day, and there are all kinds of hackers trying

---

[54] https://www.nbcnews.com/tech/security/chinese-hackers-covid-fraud-millions-rcna59636

to benefit off your data. So if you want to carve out some freedom and security in your digital life, you need to learn how to protect your privacy.

As I said, our data is forever. So it's important we take steps to protect it.

NBTV

This book is an introduction to the material that you'll find on NBTV, a channel that provides video tutorials on how to help people live a more free life in the digital age, reclaiming control of their data, money, and free online expression.

They say that the future is already here — it's just not very evenly distributed.

NBTV aims to show our growing audience that future, empowering them and giving them actionable steps they can take TODAY to live a more free life in the digital age.

While the world seems to be descending with increasing censorship and control, the reality is that there already exist tools to give us back our online freedom. There are tools to help us reclaim privacy online, to allow us to express ourselves freely without censorship, and to enable us to participate in an open and inclusive economy that's not at the whim of bureaucrats. NBTV teaches people how to use these tools, and in the process teaches them about the importance of self-ownership.

We expose people to ideas that lie outside mainstream thought, without alienating them. We aim to shape culture, celebrate human achievement, and enable our viewers, so that they can reach the maximum potential freedom in their lives.

About The Author

Naomi Brockwell is a tech journalist, and creator of "NBTV" -- a channel to help people reclaim control of their lives in the digital age. She hosts some of the largest blockchain and economics conferences around the world, and is a regular on US National TV discussing blockchain technology and current events.

From 2013 - 2015 she worked as a policy associate at the New York Bitcoin Center. Since 2015 she has worked as a producer for 19-times Emmy-Award-Winning Journalist John Stossel. From 2021 to 2022 she hosted the CoinDesk series "Break it Down", and the CoinDesk daily show "The Hash".

Naomi was a producer for the 2015 feature documentary Bitcoin: The End of Money as We Know It (Best International Documentary, Anthem Film Festival; Winner of Special Jury Prize, Amsterdam Film Festival), Audition (Best documentary, Lone Star Film Festival), and producer of the 2018 award-winning documentary about the housing crash The Bubble.

Naomi is the co-founder of "The Soho Forum", a NY debate series. She is on the Advisory Council at the "Mannkal Economic Education Foundation", and is author of the children's book Billy's Bitcoin.

Made in United States
Troutdale, OR
02/24/2024

17927239R00066